This graphic novel is an invitation for both children and adults. Let us thank its authors. Throughout the pages, the story of the life of St. Thérèse reveals the story of her soul and its secret for us: "Loving is giving everything away and giving oneself away."

Thérèse's "Little Way" consists of trust and love. This path of abandonment in Jesus' arms requires an open heart that lets itself be won over by the joy of the spirit of childhood. In this absolute trust in the love of the One who can do everything, St. Thérèse went through the trials of life and pursued her missionary desire to love Jesus and make people love Him.

—Father Olivier Ruffray
Rector of the St. Thérèse of Lisieux Sanctuary

STORY BY **COLINE DUPUY**

DRAWINGS BY **DAVIDE PERCONTI** AND **FRANCESCO RIZZATO**

COLORS BY **AMÉLIE LEFÈVRE** AND **CHRISTIAN LEROLLE**

TRANSLATED BY **JAMES HENRI MCMURTRIE**

THÉRÈSE OF LISIEUX

LOVING IS GIVING EVERYTHING AWAY

SOPHIA INSTITUTE PRESS

Manchester, New Hampshire

To Emmanuel Houis, secretary-general of the Sanctuary of Lisieux

To Sister Marie-Magdeleine and Sister Marie de Saint-Martin

To the hearts of children who are looking for the light

C. D.

Series Director: Jean-François Vivier

Copyright © 2020 by Groupe Elidia
Éditions Artège Jeunesse
10, rue Mercoeur — 75011 Paris
9, espace Méditerranée — 66000 Perpignan
www.editionsartege.fr
English translation copyright © 2021 by Sophia Institute Press

Thérèse of Lisieux: Love Is Giving Everything Away is a translation of
Thérèse of Lisieux: Aimer, c'est tout donner (Perpignan, France: Artège, 2020).

Printed in the United States of America. All rights reserved.

Sophia Institute Press
Box 5284, Manchester, NH 03108
1-800-888-9344

www.SophiaInstitute.com

Sophia Institute Press® is a registered trademark of Sophia Institute.

ISBN: 978-1-64413-590-7

Library of Congress Control Number: 2021949774

First printing

DIOCESE OF BAYEUX, MARCH 1898.

HERE'S THE MANUSCRIPT THAT WAS CORRECTED BY MOTHER AGNÈS OF JESUS AND THAT I PROOFREAD AT HER REQUEST, MONSIGNOR.

MY DEAR DOM MADELAINE, MAY MOTHER AGNÈS FORGIVE ME, BUT I DON'T TRUST THE FEMININE IMAGINATION . . .

WITH ALL DUE RESPECT, MONSIGNOR, AS THE ABBOT OF ST. MARTIN, (1) I CAN ASSURE YOU THAT EVERYTHING -- ABSOLUTELY EVERYTHING -- IN THIS MANUSCRIPT IS INVALUABLE.

LET'S SEE . . . I REMEMBER ST. THÉRÈSE OF THE CHILD JESUS AND THE HOLY FACE. SHE WAS ONLY A CHILD!

YET WE FIND A LEVEL OF THEOLOGY IN HER THAT THE MOST BEAUTIFUL SPIRITUAL BOOKS RARELY ATTAIN.

SO, IT'S YOU, MOTHER AGNÈS, WHO ASKED YOUR SISTER TO WRITE HER MEMOIRS?

THAT'S RIGHT. THÉRÈSE WAS AFRAID IT WOULD DISTRACT HER HEART, BUT SHE OBEYED ME. THIS WAS MORE THAN THREE YEARS AGO.

(1) FROM THE MONDAYE ABBEY IN NORMANDY.

3

ALENÇON, JANUARY 3, 1873.

WHAT DO YOU WANT, MY CHILD?

THIS IS FOR THE BABY WHO WAS BORN LAST NIGHT

SMILE AT THE DAWN, BUD THAT JUST BLOOMED. YOU'LL BE A ROSE SOMEDAY.

HER NAME IS THÉRÈSE, YOU KNOW!

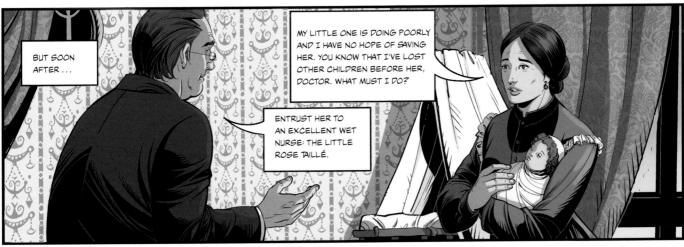

BUT SOON AFTER . . .

MY LITTLE ONE IS DOING POORLY AND I HAVE NO HOPE OF SAVING HER. YOU KNOW THAT I'VE LOST OTHER CHILDREN BEFORE HER, DOCTOR. WHAT MUST I DO?

ENTRUST HER TO AN EXCELLENT WET NURSE: THE LITTLE ROSE TAILLÉ.

AND AT THE END OF A YEAR . . .

IT'S A BEAUTIFUL BABY TANNED BY THE SUN, THAT YOU'RE GIVING ME, MY LITTLE ROSE!

AH, MRS. MARTIN, WE HAVEN'T SEEN A CUTER CHILD.

"HOW QUICKLY THOSE SUNNY YEARS OF MY CHILDHOOD PASSED BY BUT WHAT A SWEET IMPRINT THEY LEFT ON MY SOUL!"

OH, MY LITTLE CÉLINE, GIVE ME SOME BLESSED BREAD QUICKLY!

BUT I DON'T HAVE ANY THÉRÈSE. THERE WASN'T ANY MORE.

SO MAKE SOME!

PATER NOSTER, QUI ES IN CAELIS . . . (2)

PANEM NOSTRUM QUOTIDIANUM DA NOBIS HODIE . . . (3)

MY LITTLE SISTERS, I'M TOO BIG TO PLAY WITH DOLLS. THIS BASKET IS FOR YOU.

THANK YOU, LÉONIE! I WANT THIS PACKAGE OF BRAIDS . . .

AND YOU, THÉRÈSE?

ME? I CHOOSE ALL!

(2) OUR FATHER, WHO ART IN HEAVEN . . .
(3) GIVE US THIS DAY OUR DAILY BREAD . . .

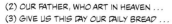

MAMA?

YES, MY LITTLE DAUGHTER?

WILL I GO TO HEAVEN?

YES MY LITTLE DAUGHTER, IF YOU ARE GOOD.

YES, BUT IF I AM NOT GOOD, I WILL GO TO HELL.... BUT I KNOW WHAT I'LL DO. I'LL FLY TO YOU IN HEAVEN. WHAT WOULD GOD BE ABLE TO DO TO TAKE ME AWAY?

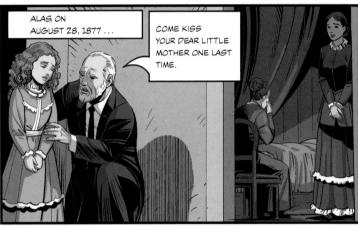

ALAS ON AUGUST 28, 1877 . . .

COME KISS YOUR DEAR LITTLE MOTHER ONE LAST TIME.

"I DON'T RECALL HAVING CRIED A LOT I SPOKE TO NOBODY ABOUT THE DEEP FEELINGS THAT FILLED MY HEART."

POOR LITTLE ONES, YOU NO LONGER HAVE A MOTHER.

WELL, MARIE WILL BE MY MOTHER.

PAULINE WILL BE MY MOTHER.

7

"DURING THE WALKS I TOOK WITH PAPA . . ."

YOU SEE, THÉRÈSE, HAPPINESS ON THIS EARTH IS TO LOVE THE CREATOR AND HIS CREATION.

PAPA, IF YOU SPOKE TO MEN IN THE GOVERNMENT THEY WOULD TAKE YOU TO MAKE YOU A KING. THEN FRANCE WOULD BE HAPPIER THAN IT'S EVER BEEN.

BUT YOU'D NO LONGER BE MY KING. SO, I PREFER THAT THEY DON'T KNOW YOU.

YES, MY LITTLE QUEEN.

"HE LIKED ME TO GIVE ALMS TO THE POOR WE MET"

HERE, GO GIVE HIM A PENNY

HERE, SIR, THIS IS FOR YOU!

NO, THANK YOU, MISS. OTHERS ARE MORE UNFORTUNATE THAN I AM.

DON'T WORRY MY LITTLE QUEEN. I'LL BUY YOU A GIFT WITH THIS PENNY.

I'LL PRAY FOR MY POOR MAN ON THE DAY OF MY FIRST COMMUNION.

LET'S GO VISIT THE BLESSED SACRAMENT IN THIS CHAPEL.

OH, PAPA, WHERE ARE WE?

IN THE CARMEL OF LISIEUX.

9

"I WAS SIX OR SEVEN YEARS OLD WHEN PAPA DROVE US TO TROUVILLE. I'LL NEVER FORGET THE IMPRESSION THE SEA MADE ON ME."

"EVERYTHING SPOKE TO MY SOUL OF THE GREATNESS AND POWER OF THE GOOD LORD."

PAPA, LOOK AT THIS SEASHELL!

IS SHE YOUR DAUGHTER? SHE'S VERY PRETTY.

SHE'S MY YOUNGEST, BUT . . .

SHH! NO COMPLIMENTS.

?

"AT NIGHT, WHEN THE SUN SEEMED TO BATHE IN THE IMMENSITY OF THE WAVES, I SAT ON A ROCK WITH PAULINE."

PAULINE, LATER, I'D LIKE TO GO AWAY WITH YOU INTO A REMOTE DESERT

MY DESIRE IS YOURS, MY THÉRÈSE. I'LL WAIT UNTIL YOU'RE OLD ENOUGH TO LEAVE.

"ONE DAY HOWEVER, THE GOOD LORD SHOWED ME A TRULY EXTRAORDINARY VISION. IT WAS THE IMAGE OF THE TRIAL THAT HE WAS PLEASED TO PREPARE FOR US IN ADVANCE."

PAPA! PAPA!

WHAT'S HAPPENING? PAPA IS ON A TRIP.

BUT I SAW HIM. HE'S OVER THERE IN THE GROVE!

WE SHOULD GO SEE, DON'T YOU THINK, MARIE?

WELL, LET'S GO. BUT YOU KNOW IT CAN'T BE PAPA!

THERE ISN'T ANYONE!

NO. NOBODY.

?!

DON'T THINK ABOUT IT ANYMORE, MY THÉRÈSE.

AND ONE DAY IN FEBRUARY 1882 ...

MARIE, I HAVE SOME NEWS TO TELL YOU ABOUT MYSELF.

TELL ME.

ARE YOU READY? I'M GOING TO ENTER THE CARMEL OF LISIEUX.

WHAT?!

"I UNDERSTOOD THAT PAULINE WAS GOING TO LEAVE ME TO GO INTO A CONVENT, THAT SHE WOULDN'T WAIT FOR ME, AND THAT I WAS GOING TO LOSE MY SECOND MOTHER."

YOU NEED TO BE IN SHAPE FOR THE CARMEL. IT'S VERY AUSTERE.

THE LORD WILL GIVE ME THE GRACE BECAUSE HE'S CALLING ME.

BOUM

THÉRÈSE! ARE YOU THERE?

OH, THÉRÈSE! DON'T CRY!

I'M LEAVING TO HIDE MYSELF IN THE DESERT BUT IT'S NOT A REMOTE DESERT, WILL YOU COME SEE ME OFTEN?

NO. I'LL FOLLOW YOU, PAULINE! I'LL ALSO BE A CARMELITE.

I'LL TALK TO THE PRIORESS MOTHER MARIE DE GONZAGUE, ABOUT IT IF YOU WISH.

"TOWARD THE END OF THE YEAR, I GOT A CONTINUAL HEADACHE. IT LASTED UNTIL EASTER OF 1883. PAPA HAD GONE TO PARIS WITH MARIE AND LÉONIE. MY AUNT TOOK CÉLINE AND ME TO HER HOME."

YOU DON'T MISS PAULINE TOO MUCH?

YES BUT WITH TIME, WE GET USED TO HER ABSENCE.

POOR CHILDREN, THIS WOULD BE A LESS PAINFUL TRIAL IF YOU STILL HAD YOUR DEAR MOTHER. MY SISTER ZÉLIE WAS AN ANGEL. HERE, I'LL TELL YOU A STORY . . .

"THAT EVENING, WE WERE TO GO TO THE CATHOLIC CIRCLE. BUT THINKING I WAS TIRED, MY AUNT HAD ME GO TO BED. WHILE SHE WAS UNDRESSING ME, I WAS SEIZED BY A STRANGE TREMOR."

NO . . . AUNT . . . CÉLINE . . .

ARE YOU COLD, THÉRÈSE?

A FEW DAYS LATER.

BA . . . BA . . . A . . . BA . . .

SHE'S DELIRIOUS, PAPA.

AND THE DOCTOR HASN'T FOUND ANYTHING. ALAS, I HOPE SHE'S NOT GOING TO GO CRAZY -- OR WORSE, THAT WE AREN'T GOING TO LOSE HER. MY POOR LITTLE GIRL LOOKS AS IF SHE HAS LOST HER SENSES.

HAVE A NOVENA OF MASSES SAID TO OUR LADY OF VICTORIES IN PARIS.

ALL RIGHT, PAPA. I'LL TAKE CARE OF IT.

"BUT THIS SICKNESS WOULD NOT LEAD TO MY DEATH. IT WAS LIKE LAZARUS'S IN ORDER FOR GOD TO BE GLORIFIED."

MAMA! MAMA!

MAMA! MAMA!

YOUR GODMOTHER IS HERE, LITTLE THÉRÈSE.

MAMA! MA . . . MA!

COME, LÉONIE. LET'S PRAY IT'S THE ONLY THING TO DO.

MA . . . MA . . .

AVE MARIA, GRATIA PLENA . . . (4)

MARIE!

THÉRÈSE?

?!

SANCTA MARIA, MATER DEI . . . (5)

I'M HEALED!

OH, THÉRÈSE! WHAT HAPPENED?

SHE SMILED AT ME. SHE WAS SO BEAUTIFUL. . . . OH, IF YOU ONLY KNEW! I'VE NEVER SEEN ANYTHING SO BEAUTIFUL!

(4) HAIL MARY FULL OF GRACE . . .
(5) HOLY MARY MOTHER OF GOD . . .

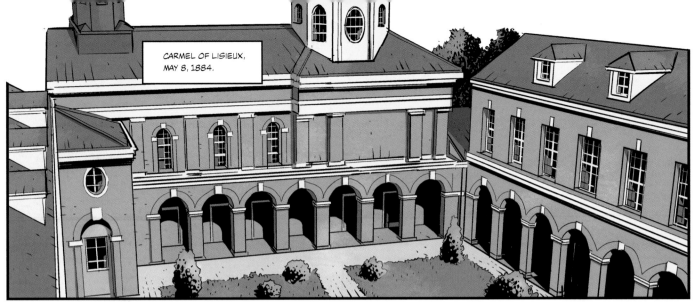

CARMEL OF LISIEUX, MAY 8, 1884.

SO, MY THÉRÈSE? HOW DID YOUR FIRST COMMUNION GO THIS MORNING?

I CRIED WITH JOY. IT WAS A KISS OF LOVE. I FELT LOVED AND SAID, "I LOVE YOU. I GIVE MYSELF TO YOU FOREVER!"

IT'S A GREAT JOY FOR ME ALSO. HERE I AM TODAY -- THE FIANCÉE OF THE KING OF KINGS, WITH THIS NEW NAME: AGNÈS OF JESUS! LET'S THINK OF THE VICTORY OF JOAN OF ARC IN ORLÉANS.

DO YOU STILL WANT TO JOIN ME IN THE DESERT?

OH YES, PAULINE! I'M JUST WAITING FOR THAT DAY

OKAY I HAVE A SURPRISE FOR YOU.

MOTHER MARIE DE GONZAGUE SUGGESTS THAT YOU TAKE THE NAME THÉRÈSE OF THE CHILD JESUS.

OH, THANK YOU, MY LITTLE MOTHER! I'VE DREAMED ABOUT IT!

"I WAS HAPPY BUT I DIDN'T KNOW HOW TO PLAY THE GAMES OF MY AGE GROUP."

COME NOW, MY LITTLE DOCTOR? YOU'RE NOT PLAYING WITH THE OTHERS?

NO, FATHER.

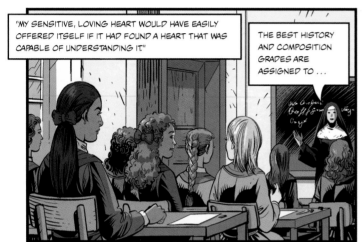

"MY SENSITIVE, LOVING HEART WOULD HAVE EASILY OFFERED ITSELF IF IT HAD FOUND A HEART THAT WAS CAPABLE OF UNDERSTANDING IT"

THE BEST HISTORY AND COMPOSITION GRADES ARE ASSIGNED TO . . .

THÉRÈSE MARTIN.

UGH! ALWAYS HER! IT'S LIKE IN CATECHISM CLASS.

"BUT ALAS. THE HEART OF CREATURES IS SO NARROW AND FICKLE!"

"I DIDN'T KNOW HOW TO PLAY I REALLY LIKED TO READ AND WOULD HAVE SPENT MY WHOLE LIFE DOING IT"

WHAT ARE YOU READING, THÉRÈSE?

THE LIFE OF JOAN OF ARC. WHAT A HEROINE! I REALLY WANT TO IMITATE HER.

"I THOUGHT THAT I WAS BORN FOR GLORY . . . MY GLORY WOULDN'T APPEAR BEFORE MORTALS. IT WOULD CONSIST OF BECOMING A GREAT SAINT! THIS DESIRE COULD SEEM RECKLESS IF ONE CONSIDERS HOW WEAK I WAS."

I'VE HEARD THAT THERE HAS NEVER BEEN A PURE SOUL THAT WAS MORE LOVING AND REPENTANT THAN MARY MAGDALENE'S. AH! HOW I'D LOVE TO BELIE THESE WORDS!

ME TOO, THÉRÈSE. I'LL BE A POOR CLARE OR A VISITANDINE NUN.

"IT WAS DURING MY SECOND HOLY COMMUNION (6) RETREAT THAT I SAW MYSELF BEING ATTACKED BY TERRIBLE SCRUPLES."

WHAT'S THE MATTER? YOU'RE CRYING SO MUCH AS A CHILD THAT LATER YOU WON'T HAVE ANY MORE TEARS TO SHED?

I'M AFRAID OF MORTAL SINS. THEY TALK TO US ABOUT THEM ALL THE TIME IN THE ABBEY. (7) DO YOU THINK I WAS SICK ON PURPOSE WHEN I COULDN'T TALK?

NO! YOUR CONDITION WAS TOO SERIOUS TO BE FAKE.

YET AM I A LIAR FOR HAVING CLAIMED TO SEE THE VIRGIN MARY SMILING AT ME?

I DON'T THINK SO. BUT TELL ME, THÉRÈSE, WHAT WILL YOU DO WHEN I'M IN THE CARMEL?

?

"WHEN I LEARNED ABOUT MARIE'S DEPARTURE, MY BEDROOM LOST ALL OF ITS ATTRACTIONS FOR ME."

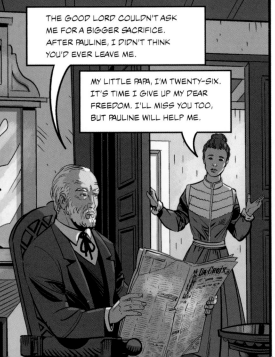

THE GOOD LORD COULDN'T ASK ME FOR A BIGGER SACRIFICE. AFTER PAULINE, I DIDN'T THINK YOU'D EVER LEAVE ME.

MY LITTLE PAPA, I'M TWENTY-SIX. IT'S TIME I GIVE UP MY DEAR FREEDOM. I'LL MISS YOU TOO, BUT PAULINE WILL HELP ME.

"A MONTH BEFORE HER ENTRANCE INTO CARMEL, PAPA DROVE US TO ALENÇON."

WHERE'S LÉONIE?

SHE'S JUST ENTERED THE POOR CLARES HERE.... LET'S NOT CALL FOR HER. SHE'S ALREADY WEARING HER POSTULANT HABIT

WHAT'S GOING ON?

!

(6) HER PROFESSION OF FAITH IN MAY 1884.
(7) THE BENEDICTINE ABBEY IN LISIEUX, WHERE THÉRÈSE ATTENDED SCHOOL.

17

"IT WAS ON DECEMBER 25, 1886, THAT I RECEIVED THE GRACE OF LEAVING MY CHILDHOOD -- IN A WORD, THE GRACE OF MY COMPLETE CONVERSION. WE WERE COMING BACK FROM MIDNIGHT MASS."

NOW THAT MARIE AND LÉONIE ARE OUT OF THE NEST, WE CAN FINALLY CELEBRATE CHRISTMAS WITHOUT CHILDISH SURPRISES! LUCKILY THIS IS THE LAST YEAR ... (8)

ARE YOU SAD, PAPA?

I'M GOING TO TAKE OFF MY HAT

THÉRÈSE IS GOING TO CRY AGAIN.

OH, THÉRÈSE! DON'T GO DOWNSTAIRS, IT WOULD CAUSE YOU TOO MUCH GRIEF TO LOOK AT YOUR SLIPPERS RIGHT NOW.

A MOMENT LATER ...

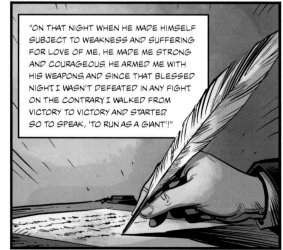

OH, THANK YOU, PAPA! YOU SPOILED ME SO MUCH ON THIS LAST CHRISTMAS EVE!

?!

HA, HA, MY LITTLE QUEEN!

"ON THAT NIGHT WHEN HE MADE HIMSELF SUBJECT TO WEAKNESS AND SUFFERING FOR LOVE OF ME, HE MADE ME STRONG AND COURAGEOUS, HE ARMED ME WITH HIS WEAPONS AND SINCE THAT BLESSED NIGHT I WASN'T DEFEATED IN ANY FIGHT, ON THE CONTRARY I WALKED FROM VICTORY TO VICTORY AND STARTED, SO TO SPEAK, 'TO RUN AS A GIANT'!"

(8) TO MR. MARTIN, THÉRÈSE, WHO WAS ALMOST FOURTEEN, WAS TOO OLD TO RECEIVE GIFTS IN HER SHOES.

ON PENTECOST IN 1887.

WHAT'S THE MATTER, MY LITTLE QUEEN?

PAPA . . .

PAPA, I DON'T WANT TO HURT YOU, BUT WILL YOU LET ME ENTER CARMEL . . . WHEN I'M FIFTEEN?

YOU'RE VERY YOUNG TO BE MAKING SUCH A SERIOUS DECISION.

OH, PAPA, IT'S AN IRRESISTIBLE CALL!

WOUF

IF YOUR DESIRE IS THAT OF GOD HIMSELF, I WON'T STAND IN THE WAY. WE'LL ASK FOR AN INTERVIEW WITH OUR BISHOP.

THE GOOD LORD REALLY HONORS ME BY ASKING ME FOR MY CHILDREN IN THIS WAY

LOOK HOW CAREFULLY THE CREATOR BROUGHT THIS LITTLE WHITE FLOWER TO LIFE AND PRESERVED IT TO THIS DAY . . . THAT IS YOUR STORY

THE FOLLOWING JULY 13...

READ ALL ABOUT IT! PRANZINI IS CONDEMNED TO DEATH!

WHO IS HE?

A NOTORIOUS CRIMINAL, MISS, AND HE REFUSES TO REPENT.

CÉLINE, HAVE YOU HEARD OF PRANZINI?

DON'T READ THAT! THIS MAN HAS COMMITTED HORRIBLE CRIMES.

CAN YOU HAVE A MASS SAID FOR HIS INTENTIONS?

WHAT? YOU WANT A MASS FOR HIM?

I WANT TO PREVENT HIM FROM FALLING INTO HELL.

OKAY I'M JOINING YOUR CAUSE.

FOR HIS SAKE, I'LL DRINK NOTHING UNTIL TOMORROW. BUT I'M ONLY ASKING FOR A SIGN OF HIS CONVERSION.

AND ON SEPTEMBER 1...

CÉLINE! HE'S SAVED!

L'Exécution de Pranzini

Révélations : l'assassin a embrassé trois fois un crucifix.

WHO?

PRANZINI! HE'S MY FIRST CHILD! I'LL BE A FISHER OF SOULS... GOD'S MERCY IS SO GREAT!

"OCTOBER 31 WAS THE DAY THAT WAS SET UP FOR MY TRIP TO BAYEUX. I WENT ALONE WITH PAPA. MY HEART WAS FILLED WITH HOPE."

MONSIGNOR HUGONIN IS WAITING FOR YOU.

HAVE YOU WANTED TO BE A CARMELITE FOR A LONG TIME?

OH, YES MONSIGNOR! FOR A VERY LONG TIME.

LET'S SEE. YOU HAVEN'T HAD THIS DESIRE FOR FIFTEEN YEARS?

THAT'S TRUE, BUT I WANTED THE CARMEL AS SOON AS I KNEW ABOUT IT

BUT YOU'RE ONLY FOURTEEN AND A HALF! TWO YEARS OF WAITING AREN'T INSURMOUNTABLE. I'M SURE YOUR FATHER AGREES WITH ME.

EXCUSE ME, MONSIGNOR. I APPROVE OF MY DAUGHTER'S REQUEST

I MUST ADMIT THAT I EVEN ENCOURAGED HER TO PUT UP HER HAIR TO MAKE HERSELF LOOK OLDER.

NEVER HAS THE LIKE BEEN SEEN BEFORE: A FATHER AS EAGER TO GIVE HIS CHILD TO GOD AS THIS CHILD IS TO OFFER HERSELF TO HIM!

ALAS I CAN'T GRANT MY PERMISSION WITHOUT THAT OF THE CARMEL'S SUPERIOR. I WON'T HIDE FROM YOU THAT YOUR WISH IS DIFFICULT TO GRANT BUT I PROMISE TO TALK TO HIM ABOUT IT

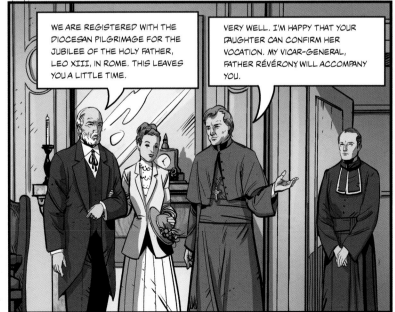

WE ARE REGISTERED WITH THE DIOCESAN PILGRIMAGE FOR THE JUBILEE OF THE HOLY FATHER, LEO XIII, IN ROME. THIS LEAVES YOU A LITTLE TIME.

VERY WELL. I'M HAPPY THAT YOUR DAUGHTER CAN CONFIRM HER VOCATION. MY VICAR-GENERAL, FATHER RÉVÉRONY WILL ACCOMPANY YOU.

"ON NOVEMBER 7, THE PILGRIMAGE LEFT FOR PARIS, BUT PAPA DROVE US INTO THIS CITY A FEW DAYS BEFORE SO THAT WE COULD VISIT IT."

AND HERE IS OUR LADY OF VICTORIES!

THE VIRGIN MARY MADE ME FEEL THAT IT WAS REALLY SHE WHO SMILED AT ME AND HEALED ME.

GOOD. I DIDN'T DOUBT IT!

"BEFORE ARRIVING IN THE ETERNAL CITY, THE GOAL OF OUR PILGRIMAGE, WE WERE ALLOWED TO SEE MANY SIGHTS."

MILAN

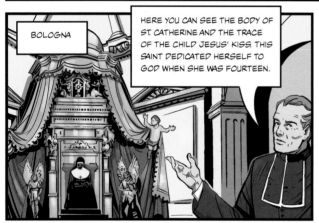

BOLOGNA

HERE YOU CAN SEE THE BODY OF ST. CATHERINE AND THE TRACE OF THE CHILD JESUS' KISS. THIS SAINT DEDICATED HERSELF TO GOD WHEN SHE WAS FOURTEEN.

LORETO

I PUT MY ROSARY IN THE CHILD JESUS' LITTLE BOWL.

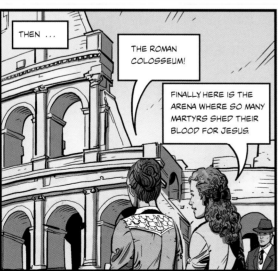

THEN ...

THE ROMAN COLOSSEUM!

FINALLY HERE IS THE ARENA WHERE SO MANY MARTYRS SHED THEIR BLOOD FOR JESUS.

COME QUICKLY! WE'LL BE ABLE TO GO THROUGH!

WHAT DO YOU WANT TO DO?

TO KISS THE GROUND AND ASK FOR THE GRACE OF MARTYRDOM.

?!

"ON SUNDAY NOVEMBER 20, AFTER HAVING DRESSED ACCORDING TO THE VATICAN PROTOCOL..."

SPEAK!

MOST HOLY FATHER, I HAVE A GREAT GRACE TO ASK OF YOU!

MOST HOLY FATHER, IN HONOR OF YOUR JUBILEE, LET ME ENTER CARMEL AT THE AGE OF FIFTEEN!

I DON'T UNDERSTAND VERY WELL.

MOST HOLY FATHER, SHE'S A CHILD WHO WANTS TO ENTER CARMEL AT THE AGE OF FIFTEEN. BUT THE SUPERIORS ARE EXAMINING THE QUESTION AT THE MOMENT

WELL, MY CHILD, DO WHAT THE SUPERIORS TELL YOU TO DO.

OH, MOST HOLY FATHER, IF YOU SAID YES, EVERYONE WOULD BE WILLING.

COME, COME! YOU'LL ENTER IF THE GOOD LORD WANTS IT!

YOU HAVEN'T HELPED THÉRÈSE MUCH IN HER DIFFICULT UNDERTAKING.

WE DON'T SEE THIS IN ITALY.

IT ISN'T MY ROLE, MR. MARTIN. NONETHELESS, YOUR DAUGHTER SEEMS SO DETERMINED THAT I'LL TRY TALKING ABOUT IT TO OUR BISHOP.

"WE HAD HARDLY ARRIVED IN LISIEUX. OUR FIRST VISIT WAS TO THE CARMEL."

I DID ALL THAT DEPENDED ON ME -- EVEN TALKING TO THE HOLY FATHER . . .

WRITE TO MONSIGNOR HUGONIN TO REMIND HIM OF HIS PROMISE.

"FINALLY TWO DAYS BEFORE CHRISTMAS MY LETTER WENT OUT I WAS CONVINCED THAT THE ANSWER WOULD COME WITHOUT DELAY. EVERY MORNING, I WENT TO THE POST OFFICE AFTER MASS WITH PAPA."

YOU DON'T HAVE A LETTER FOR ME?

NO, MISS. NOTHING YET.

"I PASSED THE AFTERNOON OF THE RADIANT FEAST IN TEARS. I WAS GOING TO SEE THE CARMELITES. THEY HAD A BIG SURPRISE FOR ME."

MERRY CHRISTMAS, MY THÉRÈSE!

OH, THANK YOU, MY SISTERS! DESPITE MY IMPATIENCE, I DREAM OF BEING A LITTLE USELESS TOY IN THE HAND OF THE CHILD JESUS.

AND ON JANUARY 1, 1888 . . .

PAPA! PAULINE GOT A RESPONSE FROM MONSIGNOR HUGONIN!

SO, WHAT IS THE ANSWER?

OH, PAPA! I'M GOING TO ENTER CARMEL AT EASTER!

"MONDAY APRIL 9, WAS THE DAY THE CARMEL CELEBRATED THE FEAST OF THE ANNUNCIATION, POSTPONED BECAUSE OF LENT THE FEAST WAS CHOSEN FOR MY ENTRANCE."

PAPA, WILL YOU BLESS ME?

RECEIVE MY BLESSING, MY LITTLE QUEEN.

WELCOME HOME, THÉRÈSE!

I AM HERE FOREVER.

THIS IS MOTHER GENEVIÈVE, THE FOUNDRESS OF OUR CARMEL.

LET ME KISS YOU, MY LITTLE DAUGHTER.

MY DAUGHTER, GIVE ME THE REASONS FOR YOUR ENTRANCE INTO THE CARMEL.

I HAVE COME TO SAVE SOULS AND, ABOVE ALL, TO PRAY FOR PRIESTS.

VERY GOOD, BUT DON'T BE PROUD OF IT

ONE MORNING . . .

I CAN TELL THAT OUR CLOISTERS ARE BEING SWEPT BY A FIFTEEN-YEAR-OLD CHILD! IT'S A PITY!

GO REMOVE THIS SPIDER WEB, AND BE MORE CAREFUL IN THE FUTURE.

LATER . . .

OH, THIS CHILD DOES ABSOLUTELY NOTHING!

MY REVEREND MOTHER, (9) THE RHYTHM OF THE DUTIES IS DIFFICULT FOR HER. . . . WE'LL BE ABLE TO EXCUSE HER FROM MATINS.

A SOUL OF THIS CALIBER MUST NOT BE TREATED LIKE A CHILD. GOD WILL SUSTAIN HER. IF SHE'S SICK, SHE MUST TELL ME HERSELF.

(9) MOTHER MARIE DE GONZAGUE.

"HOWEVER, THE TIME OF MY RECEIVING THE HABIT HAD ARRIVED.... MONSIGNOR SCHEDULED THE CEREMONY FOR JANUARY 10."

AH! THERE'S MY LITTLE QUEEN!

COME. LET'S THANK THE LORD FOR THE HONOR THAT HE GIVES ME OF CHOOSING SPOUSES IN MY HOUSE.

YOUR NAME IS NOW SISTER THÉRÈSE OF THE CHILD JESUS AND THE HOLY FACE.

TE DEUM LAUDAMUS ... (10)

MONSIGNOR, THIS CANTICLE IS SUNG ONLY DURING PROFESSIONS ...

NO MATTER! THIS FEAST IS UNIQUE. MY LITTLE DAUGHTER HAS BECOME A CARMELITE.

TE DOMINUM CONFITEMUR! (11)

(10) WE PRAISE YOU, O GOD.
(11) WE BLESS YOU, LORD.

"I DIDN'T KNOW THAT ON FEBRUARY 12, A MONTH AFTER MY TAKING MY HABIT, OUR DEAR FATHER WAS GOING TO DRINK FROM THE BITTEREST AND MOST HUMILIATING OF ALL CHALICES."

PAPA IS SEIZED BY HALLUCINATIONS. HE HAS BEEN COMMITTED TO THE BON SAUVEUR IN CAEN. UNCLE ISIDORE HAD TO TAKE HIS REVOLVER AWAY FROM HIM. HE THOUGHT HE HAD TO DEFEND ME.

!

TELL ME IT'S NOT TRUE.

IT'S REALLY TRUE, MARIE. IT'S THE BIGGEST TRIAL THAT COULD HAVE HAPPENED TO US.

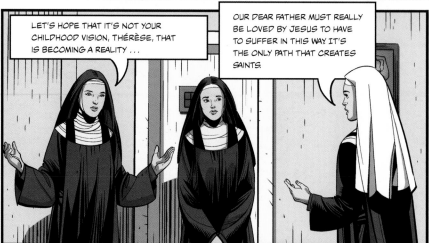

LET'S HOPE THAT IT'S NOT YOUR CHILDHOOD VISION, THÉRÈSE, THAT IS BECOMING A REALITY . . .

OUR DEAR FATHER MUST REALLY BE LOVED BY JESUS TO HAVE TO SUFFER IN THIS WAY. IT'S THE ONLY PATH THAT CREATES SAINTS.

THE WORST THING IS THAT HE HAD TO SIGN A WAIVER FOR ALL HIS PROPERTY. LÉONIE AND I WILL NO LONGER BE ABLE TO STAY AT THE BUISSONNETS AT CHRISTMAS. THE GUÉRINS WILL RECEIVE US IN THEIR HOME.

AND WHAT WILL HAPPEN TO OUR FURNITURE?

MUCH OF IT WILL BE GIVEN TO THE CARMEL . . .

EVEN THE STATUE OF OUR LADY OF THE SMILE?

YES, DEAR THÉRÈSE. IT'S FOR YOU!

LÉONIE WILL HELP ME WITH THE MOVE EVEN IF SHE'S STILL DREAMING ABOUT RECEIVING THE HABIT

SHE'LL RECEIVE IT. JESUS IS WAITING FOR HER . . .

POOR LÉONIE . . .

LET'S PRAY FOR HER. IT MAY BE DIFFICULT FOR HER TO RECOVER FROM A NEW FAILURE -- AFTER LEAVING THE POOR CLARES AND THE VISITATION.

"I RECALL AN ACT OF CHARITY THAT THE GOOD LORD INSPIRED ME TO DO WHILE I WAS STILL A NOVICE. IT WASN'T MUCH."

WOULD YOU LIKE ME TO HELP YOU TO THE REFECTORY SISTER SAINT-PIERRE?

NO! I KNOW HOW TO MANAGE!

OKAY, HELP ME.

MERCY! YOU'RE GOING TOO FAST I'M GOING TO COLLAPSE.

FOLLOW ME. I DON'T FEEL YOUR HAND ANYMORE. YOU LET IT GO. I'M GOING TO FALL!

HERE, MY SISTER. YOU CAN HAVE YOUR SUPPER.

DO YOU WANT ME TO HELP YOU CUT YOUR BREAD?

NO! LEAVE ME ALONE!

IT'S BADLY CUT! YOU DON'T KNOW HOW TO DO ANYTHING!

IT'S TRUE, MY SISTER. FORGIVE ME!

THE NEXT MORNING.

DO YOU WANT MILK IN YOUR PORRIDGE, MY SISTER?

WHY ARE YOU SMILING AT ME?

BECAUSE I'M HAPPY TO SEE YOU!

"NOT A SINGLE DOUBT HAD YET OCCURRED TO ME ABOUT MY VOCATION. I HAD TO KNOW THIS TRIAL."

WHAT MUST I DO, MY GOD? HAVEN'T I WAITED ALL MY LIFE FOR THIS SEPTEMBER 8?

MOTHER GENEVIÈVE . . .

COME IN, SISTER THÉRÈSE, COME SEE ME.

MY MOTHER, TOMORROW, I'LL BE THE SPOUSE OF THE ONE WHOSE FACE IS HIDDEN FROM ME. IS THIS WHY I'M DOUBTING MY VOCATION?

REMAIN IN PEACE.

REMEMBER, MY CHILD, THAT OUR GOD IS THE GOD OF PEACE.

KNOW THAT I ALSO DOUBTED THE DAY BEFORE MY PROFESSION . . .

OH MY MOTHER, YOU'RE SO GOOD. . . . YOU WON'T GO TO PURGATORY.

I HOPE SO. . . . I LEAVE MY HEART TO YOU.

MAY 12, 1892.

THERE! THANKS TO UNCLE ISIDORE, ALL YOUR DAUGHTERS ARE GATHERED AROUND YOU!

I BROUGHT YOU SOME FISH.

HOW ARE YOU, PAPA?

!

NO, PAPA, LET'S SEE . . .

DON'T WORRY IT'S NORMAL . . .

HOW CAN WE COMPLAIN WHEN JESUS HIMSELF WAS CONSIDERED TO BE A MAN WHO WAS STRUCK BY GOD AND HUMILIATED?

I REFUSED A THIRD MARRIAGE PROPOSAL AT THE LAST PARTY. MY DANCE PARTNER WASN'T ABLE TO DANCE. HE WAS SUDDENLY PARALYZED!

DON'T GO LOOKING. JESUS WANTS YOU FOR HIMSELF, LÉONIE . . .

HOW DO YOU KNOW, THÉRÈSE?

I HOPE SO.

GOODBYE, PAPA!

YOU'LL SEE US AGAIN SOON?

IN HEAVEN!

GO TO GOD, MY KING. . . . FAREWELL, HOLY FACE OF MY CRUCIFIED ONE.

"MY NINETEENTH BIRTHDAY WAS MARKED BY A DEATH THAT WAS SOON FOLLOWED BY TWO OTHERS."

IT LOOKS AS IF OUR POOR MOTHER GENEVIÈVE STARTED THE BALL ROLLING FOR THE VICTIMS OF THIS FLU EPIDEMIC.... WE'RE LUCKY NOT TO HAVE BEEN AFFECTED BY IT!

YES, SISTER MARIE, (12) THE SACRED HEART IS PROTECTING YOU! BUT LET US REJOICE FOR OUR DYING PEOPLE. THEY ARE GOING TO A BETTER LIFE.

AND THEN, IN FEBRUARY 1893 ...

MY SISTERS, BEFORE ELECTING THE NEW PRIORESS AFTER THE MOURNING OF THE COMMUNITY, I WANT TO INFORM YOU THAT MOTHER GENEVIÈVE INDICATED HER PREFERENCE TO ME BEFORE LEAVING US ...

"ON THAT DAY PAULINE BECAME MY LIVING JESUS. SHE BECAME 'MOTHER' FOR THE SECOND TIME!"

I THANK YOU, MY SISTERS, FOR GIVING ME THIS HONOR. I'LL TRY TO SHOW MYSELF WORTHY OF IT

IN ACCORDANCE WITH TRADITION, I NAME MOTHER MARIE DE GONZAGUE NOVICE MISTRESS.

BUT ALLOW ME TO HAVE SISTER THÉRÈSE OF THE CHILD JESUS AND THE HOLY FACE JOIN HER. I TRUST HER DISCERNMENT

(12) SISTER OF THÉRÈSE, WHO BECAME MARIE OF THE SACRED HEART

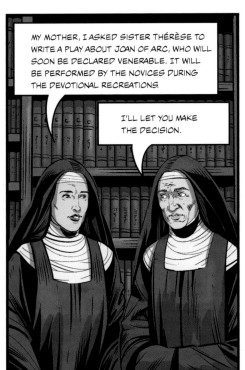

MY MOTHER, I ASKED SISTER THÉRÈSE TO WRITE A PLAY ABOUT JOAN OF ARC, WHO WILL SOON BE DECLARED VENERABLE. IT WILL BE PERFORMED BY THE NOVICES DURING THE DEVOTIONAL RECREATIONS.

I'LL LET YOU MAKE THE DECISION.

"THE GOOD LORD SHOWED ME THE SAME MERCY THAT HE SHOWED KING SOLOMON. HE DIDN'T WANT ME TO HAVE A SINGLE DESIRE THAT WASN'T FULFILLED -- NOT ONLY MY DESIRES FOR PERFECTION, BUT EVEN THOSE WHOSE VANITY I UNDERSTOOD WITHOUT HAVING EXPERIENCED IT"

THERE, MY MOTHER, IT'S A PLAY ABOUT HER MISSION. I DARE TO HOPE THAT IT WILL BE GOOD FOR SOULS.

YOU'LL PLAY THE MAIN ROLE -- THAT OF JOAN. IT WILL BE MY FEAST DAY.

JANUARY 21, 1894, ST. AGNES'S FEAST DAY

"OH, FRANCE! OH, MY BEAUTIFUL HOMELAND! WE HAVE TO LIFT YOU UP TO THE HEAVENS IF YOU WANT TO FIND LIFE AGAIN. MAY YOUR NAME BE GLORIOUS!"

"THE GOD OF THE FRANKS IN HIS MERCY RESOLVED TO SAVE YOU. BUT HE STILL WANTS TO REDEEM YOU THROUGH ME -- JOAN OF ARC."

"COME TO ME, BEAUTIFUL HOMELAND! I PRAY FOR YOU. MY VOICE IS CALLING YOU. RETURN TO ME!"

CAREFUL!

WE'LL SAVE YOU, SISTER THÉRÈSE!

I'M IN JESUS' ARMS.

SISTER THÉRÈSE IS REALLY COMPOSED!

DO YOU WANT TO KNOW WHAT I THINK? EXCEPT FOR THIS LAST SCENE, THIS PLAY ONLY SERVES TO MAINTAIN HER PRIDE.

33

JULY 30, 1894.

I BROUGHT A NOTE FOR YOU, MY REVEREND MOTHER.

Papa est au Ciel. J'ai reçu son dernier soupir. Je lui ai fermé les yeux. Son beau visage a pris aussitôt une expression de béatitude.

Céline

THÉRÈSE, CÉLINE JUST TOLD ME THAT PAPA . . .

HIS DEATH DOESN'T FEEL LIKE DEATH TO ME, BUT A TRUE LIFE. . . . IN HEAVEN WE WILL FIND THE FATHER AND MOTHER WHO OFFERED US TO JESUS.

"FINALLY MY DEAR KING HASTENED TO SORT OUT HIS CÉLINE'S MUDDLED AFFAIRS AND SHE JOINED US ON SEPTEMBER 14!"

WHAT IS CÉLINE GOING TO DO?

THE GUÉRINS THINK THAT SHE DOESN'T HAVE A VOCATION. BUT SHE WANTS TO JOIN US. IT WOULD BE THE FIRST TIME IN THE HISTORY OF CARMEL THAT FOUR SISTERS WOULD BE IN THE SAME HOUSE.

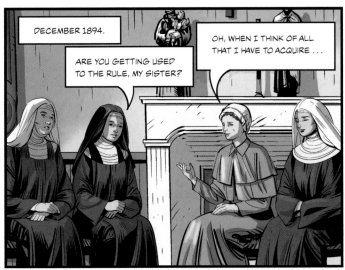

DECEMBER 1894.

ARE YOU GETTING USED TO THE RULE, MY SISTER?

OH, WHEN I THINK OF ALL THAT I HAVE TO ACQUIRE . . .

SAY "TO LOSE" INSTEAD! JESUS WILL FILL YOUR SOUL WITH SPLENDOR AS YOU RID IT OF ITS IMPERFECTIONS.

BUT THERE ARE OBSTACLES THAT SEEM INSURMOUNTABLE TO ME. . . . I COULDN'T OVERCOME THEM!

THAT DOESN'T SURPRISE ME. WE'RE TOO LITTLE TO RISE ABOVE OUR DIFFICULTIES. WE HAVE TO GO UNDERNEATH THEM.

DO YOU RECALL THE HORSE WE HAD TO GO UNDER WHEN WE WERE LITTLE BECAUSE HE BLOCKED OUR WAY?

YES I REMEMBER. YOU HAVE SUCH TRUST . . .

WELL, TO APPROACH JESUS, IT'S THE SAME THING. YOU HAVE TO BE SO SMALL! THE BELOVED NEEDS NEITHER OUR BRILLIANT WORKS NOR OUR BEAUTIFUL THOUGHTS. HE CHERISHES SIMPLICITY.

MOTHER AGNÈS, YOU SHOULD ASK HER TO WRITE HER REMEMBRANCES. WITHOUT THAT, THEY WILL BE LOST TO US!

DO YOU THINK SO, MY SISTER? (13) THAT ISN'T DONE IN THE CARMEL, UNLESS IT'S USED SOMEDAY FOR HER OBITUARY . . .

THÉRÈSE HAS SO MANY THINGS TO TEACH US. . . . SHE'S AN ANGEL WHO WON'T STAY ON EARTH FOR LONG. AND HASN'T SHE SHOWN US THAT SHE'S THE COMMUNITY'S POET?

SISTER THÉRÈSE! COME HERE. I HAVE SOMETHING TO ASK YOU.

YES MY MOTHER?

(13) SISTER MARIE OF THE SACRED HEART.

35

FEBRUARY 1895.

HERE, MY SISTER. IT WAS OUR FATHER'S CAMERA. BUT IT STILL WORKS.

I'M REALLY GOING TO LOVE CALLING YOU SISTER GENEVIÈVE OF THE HOLY FACE.

STRIKE A POSE!

HOLD STILL.

ON JUNE 11 . . .

PSST! SISTER GENEVIÈVE OF THE HOLY FACE!

YES, SISTER THÉRÈSE?

WOULD YOU LIKE TO OFFER YOURSELF WITH ME AS A VICTIM OF HOLOCAUST TO MERCIFUL LOVE? I WROTE A PRAYER THAT MOTHER AGNÈS AUTHORIZED US TO SAY.

?!

HAVE YOU WEIGHED THE CONSEQUENCES OF SUCH A WISH? SOULS WHO OFFER THEMSELVES AS VICTIMS DRAW PUNISHMENTS ON THEMSELVES THAT ARE RESERVED FOR THE GUILTY.

BUT IT'S VERY DIFFERENT TO OFFER YOURSELF TO DIVINE JUSTICE. THERE'S NOTHING TO FEAR FROM THE OFFERING TO MERCIFUL LOVE, FOR WE CAN EXPECT ONLY MERCY FROM THIS LOVE.

OKAY, I TRUST YOU. LET'S GO.

"IN ORDER TO LIVE IN ONE SINGLE ACT OF PERFECT LOVE, I OFFER MYSELF AS A VICTIM OF HOLOCAUST TO YOUR MERCIFUL LOVE, ASKING YOU TO CONSUME ME INCESSANTLY, ALLOWING THE WAVES OF INFINITE TENDERNESS SHUT UP WITHIN YOU TO OVERFLOW INTO MY SOUL . . ."

"NOW, I HAVE NO OTHER DESIRE THAN TO LOVE JESUS. MY NATURE IS SUCH THAT FEAR MAKES ME SHRINK, WHILE, UNDER LOVE'S SWEET RULE, I NOT ONLY ADVANCE -- I FLY!"

MY GOD, I KNOW THAT PICKING UP A PIN OUT OF LOVE CAN CONVERT A SOUL. HERE'S ONE!

SISTER THÉRÈSE, I RECEIVED THIS LETTER FROM A TWENTY-ONE-YEAR-OLD SEMINARIAN -- MAURICE BELLIÈRE. HE'S ASKING ONE OF US TO HELP HIM.

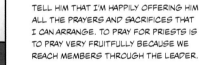

DO YOU WANT TO FULFILL THIS MISSION?

YOU'RE FULFILLING ME, MOTHER AGNÈS! I'VE HAD THIS DESIRE TO HAVE A BROTHER PRIEST FOR A LONG TIME. BUT IT SEEMED COMPLETELY UNACHIEVABLE. I GLADLY ACCEPT!

TELL HIM THAT I'M HAPPILY OFFERING HIM ALL THE PRAYERS AND SACRIFICES THAT I CAN ARRANGE. TO PRAY FOR PRIESTS IS TO PRAY VERY FRUITFULLY BECAUSE WE REACH MEMBERS THROUGH THE LEADER.

VERY GOOD, YOU CAN RESPOND IN WRITING WHEN I AUTHORIZE YOU TO DO IT

"HOW WILL SHE FINISH THIS STORY OF A LITTLE WHITE FLOWER? IT MAY BE GATHERED IN ITS FRESHNESS OR TRANSPLANTED ON OTHER SHORES ... I DON'T KNOW. BUT I KNOW THAT THE GOOD LORD'S MERCY WILL ALWAYS ACCOMPANY IT"

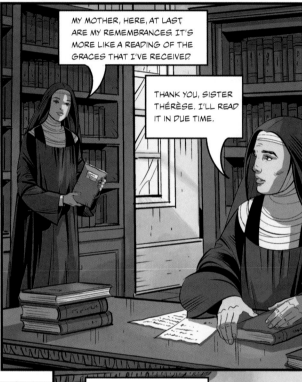

MY MOTHER, HERE, AT LAST, ARE MY REMEMBRANCES. IT'S MORE LIKE A READING OF THE GRACES THAT I'VE RECEIVED.

THANK YOU, SISTER THÉRÈSE. I'LL READ IT IN DUE TIME.

OH, HOW UPSET I WOULD BE TO HAVE READ ALL THESE BOOKS!

WHY? IT WOULD BE A GAIN, NOT A LOSS.

I WOULD HAVE WASTED PRECIOUS TIME THAT I COULD HAVE EMPLOYED SIMPLY IN LOVING GOD. I LEAVE THE BEAUTIFUL BOOKS THAT I CAN'T UNDERSTAND TO GREAT MINDS, SINCE ONLY THE HEARTS OF CHILDREN WILL BE ADMITTED TO THE HEAVENLY BANQUET.

AND YET YOU READ THE WRITINGS OF ST. JOHN OF THE CROSS?

THAT'S TRUE. BUT WHAT WILL I FIND THAT'S BETTER? HE UNDERSTOOD THAT LOVE KNOWS HOW TO TAKE ADVANTAGE OF THE GOOD AS WELL AS THE EVIL THAT IT FINDS IN US.

FEBRUARY 1896.

THE CHAPTER MEETING TODAY IS TO DECIDE ON THE ADMISSION OF THE PROFESSION OF SISTER GENEVIÈVE OF THE HOLY FACE.... OUR COUSIN MARIE SHOULD TAKE THE HABIT AT THE SAME TIME AS SHE.

MY SISTERS, IT SEEMS TO ME, AS THE FORMER PRIORESS THAT IT WOULD BE INAPPROPRIATE FOR THE MARTIN SISTERS TO DECIDE ON THE FUTURE OF SISTER GENEVIÈVE. I ASK THAT THIS MEETING BE HELD WITHOUT THEM.

?!

IT'S UNBELIEVABLE. WHAT NERVE!

A REAL SNAKE!

MOTHER MARIE DE GONZAGUE HAS RESOLVED TO SEND SISTER GENEVIÈVE OF THE HOLY FACE TO THE CARMEL IN SAIGON. SHE'S AFRAID THAT OUR FAMILIAL "CLAN" THREATENS THE SPIRIT OF CARMEL.

SHE HAS THE RIGHT TO TEST SISTER GENEVIÈVE.

IT'S A KIND OF TEST THAT SHOULDN'T BE IMPOSED?

FINALLY . . .

I'M ADMITTED TO THE PROFESSION! I'M STAYING WITH YOU.

A FEW WEEKS LATER . . .

WE'RE IN THE SIXTH ROUND OF VOTING -- THE SEVENTH ROUND CURRENTLY.

YOU'VE BEEN REELECTED PRIORESS MOTHER MARIE DE GONZAGUE.

WELL . . . I'LL ALSO KEEP THE TASK OF NOVICE MISTRESS. BUT I'LL TAKE SISTER THÉRÈSE OF THE CHILD JESUS AS MY ASSISTANT.

"NONETHELESS, ON GOOD FRIDAY JESUS WANTED TO GIVE ME THE HOPE OF SEEING HIM SOON IN HEAVEN."

"I VERY ENTHUSIASTICALLY ATTENDED THE PRIME PRAYER MEETING AND THE CHAPTER OF GRACE."

MY MOTHER, I ASK YOU TO FORGIVE ME FOR ALL THE PAIN I'VE CAUSED YOU AND THAT I'LL CAUSE YOU AGAIN. I SPIT OUT SOME BLOOD TONIGHT BUT I'M NOT SUFFERING AT ALL. DON'T GIVE ME ANYTHING.

ARE YOU SURE? I'M GOING TO HAVE YOUR COUSIN DR. LA NÉELE COME SECRETLY.

I'M SORRY BUT I CAN'T EVALUATE YOUR SYMPTOMS THROUGH A GRILLE.

IT DOESN'T MATTER, DOCTOR. HOW IS YOUR WIFE, MY DEAR JEANNE?

SHE'S DOING WELL, BUT SINCE HER SISTER JOINED YOU, SHE HAS HAD SCRUPLES ABOUT NOT HAVING BEEN INFLUENCED BY THE CALL TO THE CONVENT

I'LL PRAY TO HER VENERABLE PATRON SAINT FOR HER.

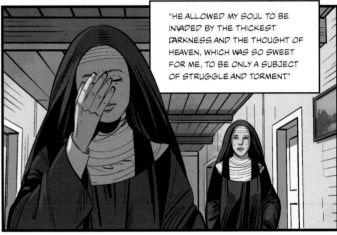

"HE ALLOWED MY SOUL TO BE INVADED BY THE THICKEST DARKNESS AND THE THOUGHT OF HEAVEN, WHICH WAS SO SWEET FOR ME, TO BE ONLY A SUBJECT OF STRUGGLE AND TORMENT."

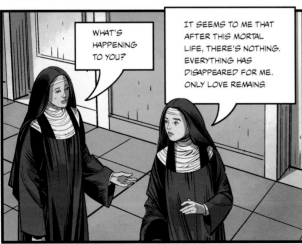

WHAT'S HAPPENING TO YOU?

IT SEEMS TO ME THAT AFTER THIS MORTAL LIFE, THERE'S NOTHING. EVERYTHING HAS DISAPPEARED FOR ME. ONLY LOVE REMAINS.

?

DON'T WORRY MY DEAR SISTER. (14) JESUS IS JUST MAKING ME UNDERSTAND THAT THERE REALLY ARE SOULS WITHOUT FAITH AND HOPE.

(14) CÉLINE, OR SISTER GENEVIÈVE OF THE HOLY FACE.

MAY 30, 1896.

SISTER THÉRÈSE, A TWENTY-SIX-YEAR-OLD FUTURE PRIEST ADOLPHE ROULLAND? NEEDS YOUR SUPPORT. HE'S INVOLVED IN THE FOREIGN MISSIONS IN PARIS.

IT WOULD BE A PLEASURE. BUT I DON'T THINK I CAN ACCEPT A SECOND SPIRITUAL BROTHER . . .

YOUR OBEDIENCE WILL DOUBLE YOUR MERITS. . . HE'LL SOON VISIT YOU AFTER HIS ORDINATION AND BEFORE LEAVING FOR CHINA.

ON THE FOLLOWING JULY 3 . . .

I'D BE VERY HAPPY TO WORK WITH YOU FOR THE SALVATION OF SOULS. ALAS, I CAN'T BE A MISSIONARY THROUGH ACTION. BUT I WANT TO BE ONE THROUGH LOVE.

OH, BUT A CARMELITE SISTER IS A GREAT MISSIONARY!

I KNOW THAT YOU'LL HAVE A LOT OF TRIALS . . .

TO BE HONEST WITH YOU, ON SEPTEMBER 8, 1890, OUR LADY FIRST SAVED MY VOCATION.

ON SEPTEMBER 8, 1890? ON THIS SAME DAY A LITTLE CARMELITE NUN BECAME THE SPOUSE OF THE KING OF HEAVEN! SHE ASKED JESUS FOR A PRIEST TO RECEIVE THE SAME GRACES AND HAVE THE SAME DESIRES AS SHE DID?

!

I THOUGHT I'D MEET THE APOSTLE -- THE BROTHER THAT I HAD SO ASKED JESUS FOR -- ONLY IN HEAVEN.

WHAT AN ASTONISHING WORK OF PROVIDENCE!

I'M GOING AWAY HAPPY BECAUSE I KNOW THAT OUR APOSTOLATE -- YOURS AND MINE -- WILL BE BLESSED BY GOD.

BEAR IN MIND THAT I'M SICK -- I WHO WOULD SO MUCH HAVE LIKED TO DIE IN AN ARENA. I'LL ASK THE GOOD LORD THAT ALL THE PRAYERS THAT ARE SAID FOR ME WOULD SERVE NOT TO ALLEVIATE MY SUFFERING BUT TO SAVE SINNERS -- YOUR SINNERS.

41

HAVE YOU OPENED SISTER THÉRÈSE'S NOTEBOOK? I'D REALLY LIKE TO READ IT

NO, BUT I'LL WILLINGLY LEND IT TO YOU, SISTER MARIE.

THANK YOU, MY DEAR SISTER! HAVE YOU NOTICED THAT SHE HAS BEEN PALE FOR A FEW WEEKS?

YOU'VE NOTICED IT TOO? I THINK OUR REVEREND MOTHER ISN'T TELLING US EVERYTHING.

I'VE READ YOUR REMEMBRANCES. YOU'RE JESUS' PRIVILEGED LITTLE SPOUSE. HE'S ENTRUSTING ALL HIS SECRETS TO YOU!

WHY DO YOU SAY THAT? THE MOST PERFECT GIFTS ARE NOTHING WITHOUT LOVE.

COUGH! COUGH! COUGH!

ARE YOU SICK? BE CAREFUL! YOU'RE GETTING SPLASHED!

IT'S NOTHING. REST ASSURED, OTHERS ARRIVE IN HEAVEN THROUGH MARTYRDOM. I DO IT THROUGH THE SPECIAL HEATER MOTHER MARIE DE GONZAGUE ORDERED FOR ME! LUCKILY ONLY LOVE AND OBEDIENCE COUNT

GRANT YOUR GODMOTHER A FAVOR: WRITE ME THE REST!

OH, WOULD YOU LIKE THAT? I'M GOING TO WRITE YOU A BEAUTIFUL LETTER.

MAY 1897.

SO, YOU'RE REALLY SICK? FOR HOW LONG HAVE YOU BEEN SPITTING UP BLOOD?

FOR MORE THAN A YEAR. BUT DON'T FEEL BAD, MY DEAR LITTLE MOTHER, THAT YOUR LITTLE DAUGHTER HAS SEEMED TO HIDE SOMETHING FROM YOU.... I WOULDN'T HAVE EVEN WANTED THE GOOD LORD TO KNOW ABOUT IT

I'D DIE OF GRIEF IF . . .

I DON'T WANT TO DIE ANY MORE THAN I WANT TO LIVE. HE'S THE ONE WHO CHOOSES! I PREFER WHAT HE WANTS EVEN IF I DON'T FEEL HIS PRESENCE ANYMORE.

JESUS, HAVING SEEN THAT, WAS INDIGNANT AND SAID TO THEM: "LET THE LITTLE CHILDREN COME TO ME, AND DO NOT STOP THEM; FOR IT IS TO SUCH AS THESE THAT THE KINGDOM OF HEAVEN BELONGS."

MY MOTHER, COULD YOU ORDER SISTER THÉRÈSE TO WRITE SOMETHING MORE SERIOUS THAN HER REMEMBRANCES NOW? TIME IS RUNNING OUT.

SO, YOU KNOW EVERYTHING? IT'S TUBERCULOSIS.

TWO MONTHS LATER.

WHAT ARE YOU WRITING THIS MORNING?

I'M WRITING A CANTICLE ABOUT THE VIRGIN MARY. IT'S TITLED "WHY I LOVE YOU, O MARY" BEFORE DYING, I'D LIKE TO EXPRESS EVERYTHING I'M THINKING ABOUT HER.

THE TIMING IS GOOD! I'M BRINGING YOU YOUR STATUE. MOTHER MARIE DE GONZAGUE AUTHORIZED ME TO BRING IT DOWN TO YOU.

I FEEL SORRY ABOUT MAKING YOU START A NEW MANUSCRIPT... BUT I'LL PROCLAIM YOUR FEATS OF ARMS. SISTER MARIE OF THE SACRED HEART NO LONGER RECOGNIZES YOU. SHE SAID YOU'RE POSSESSED BY GOD.

AS WE'LL SEE, EVERYTHING COMES FROM HIM.... I SENSE THAT MY MISSION OF HAVING HIM LOVED AS I LOVE HIM AND OF GIVING MY LITTLE WAY TO SOULS WILL START YES I WANT TO SPEND MY HEAVEN DOING GOOD ON THE EARTH.

WHAT IS YOUR LITTLE WAY?

IT'S ABOUT HAVING A BLIND TRUST IN GOD'S MERCY LIKE A CHILD WHO FEARLESSLY SLEEPS IN HIS FATHER'S ARMS.

BUT I KNOW THAT YOU HAVE SO MANY HIDDEN MERITS!

IF I HAD TRIED TO COLLECT MERITS AT THIS TIME, I'D BE DESPERATE. I'VE NEVER WANTED ANYTHING BUT TO PLEASE THE GOOD LORD AND EVEN IF I'D COMMITTED EVERY POSSIBLE CRIME, I'D ALWAYS HAVE THE SAME CONFIDENCE, FOR A MULTITUDE OF OFFENSES IS NOTHING BUT A DROP OF WATER IN THE BLAZING FIRE OF GOD'S HEART FOR THE ONE WHO REPENTS.

TELL ME WHAT HAPPENED TO YOU AFTER YOUR OFFERING TO MERCIFUL LOVE.

WELL, I STARTED MY WAY OF THE CROSS, AND THEN, SUDDENLY I WAS SEIZED BY A STRONG LOVE OF GOD, AS IF I'D BEEN COMPLETELY PLUNGED INTO THE FIRE. I BURNED WITH LOVE.

DO YOU WANT HIM?

RIGHT AWAY MY LITTLE MOTHER!

BUT IT'S HIS FACE THAT I KISS!

HERE. HE'S KISSING YOU TOO! HE LOVES YOU SO MUCH!

AUGUST 1897.

LET'S GO OUTSIDE. THE LITTLE BIRD SHOULD GO OUT

GATHER THESE ROSE PETALS MY LITTLE SISTER. YOU'LL USE THEM TO MAKE PEOPLE HAPPY LATER . . .

YOU'RE TAKING CARE OF A BABY WHO'S AT DEATH'S DOOR.

SO, YOU'RE GOING TO LEAVE ME?

OH! NOT AT ALL! I'LL COME DOWN . . .

AFTER MY DEATH, I'LL MAKE LÉONIE ENTER THE VISITATION, AND SHE'LL STAY THERE. AND WHEN PAPA ASKS ME, "WHAT DO YOU WANT, MY LITTLE DAUGHTER?," I'LL ANSWER HIM: "HAPPINESS FOR ALL THOSE I LOVE!"

PAPA OR THE GOOD LORD?

OH, YES, THE GOOD LORD IS REALLY MY FATHER. HOW SWEET IT IS TO GIVE HIM THIS NAME!

NOW, I MUST GIVE YOU ANOTHER BACK RUB. IT'S ONE OF MOTHER MARIE DE GONZAGUE'S ORDERS.

VERY WELL. WHEN I TELL YOU I'M SUFFERING, SAY "SO MUCH THE BETTER!" I DON'T HAVE THE STRENGTH, BUT YOU CAN EXPRESS MY THOUGHT FOR ME.

SEPTEMBER 30, 1897.

BUT I'M NOT SORRY FOR HAVING SURRENDERED TO LOVE. OH, NO! I'M NOT SORRY ABOUT IT!

WHAT IS AGONY? WHAT IS AGONY? I'M IN IT ALL THE TIME.... OH, MY SISTERS! HOW WE MUST PRAY FOR THE DYING! IF WE ONLY KNEW!

I WOULD NEVER HAVE THOUGHT THAT I'D SUFFER SO MUCH. I CAN ONLY EXPLAIN THIS BY THE EAGERNESS I'VE HAD TO WANT TO SAVE SOULS.

TO REFRESH YOU ...

CÉLINE ...

MY MOTHER, ISN'T THIS AGONY YET? WON'T I DIE?

YES MY POOR LITTLE ONE. BUT THE GOOD LORD MAY WANT TO PROLONG IT FOR A FEW HOURS.

AH, VERY WELL THEN ... VERY WELL ... I DO NOT WISH TO SUFFER LESS!

OPEN ALL THE DOORS!

(15) I BELIEVE IN ONE GOD . . .
(16) I WAIT FOR THE RESURRECTION OF THE DEAD . . .
(17) AND THE LIFE OF THE WORLD TO COME. AMEN.

IF ALL THIS IS TRUE, WE'RE DEALING WITH A LITTLE SAINT.

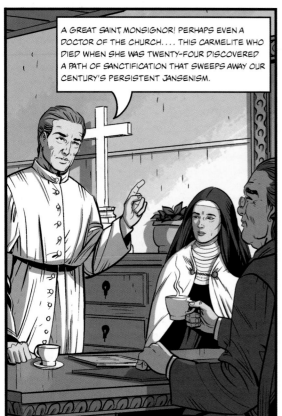

A GREAT SAINT, MONSIGNOR! PERHAPS EVEN A DOCTOR OF THE CHURCH.... THIS CARMELITE WHO DIED WHEN SHE WAS TWENTY-FOUR DISCOVERED A PATH OF SANCTIFICATION THAT SWEEPS AWAY OUR CENTURY'S PERSISTENT JANSENISM.

I BELIEVE IT ALSO.... THÉRÈSE CALLED IT HER LITTLE WAY OF CHILDHOOD -- A WAY OF TRUST AND LOVE. WITH HER, GOD WAS NO LONGER A JUDGE TO FEAR, BUT A FATHER TO LOVE.

HMM, YOU'RE VERY ENTHUSIASTIC. BUT I TRUST YOUR INTUITIONS.

AFTER ALL, I WAS HER BISHOP, AND I'M NO STRANGER TO HER EARLY ASCENT TO MOUNT CARMEL.

HAVE THIS MANUSCRIPT PUBLISHED? WHO KNOWS? A FEW HUNDRED COPIES OF IT COULD BE SOLD ...

FIN

Thérèse at thirteen years old.

Thérèse as Joan of Arc.

Thérèse, twenty-four years old, at her death.

Thérèse, her three sisters, and
Mother Marie de Gonzague on
the day Céline received her habit.

BIBLIOGRAPHY

Gaucher, Guy. *Histoire d'une vie, Thérèse Martin* [The Story of a Life: St. Thérèse of Lisieux]. Paris: Éditions du Cerf, 1998.

Thérèse of Lisieux. *Conseils et souvenirs recueillis par Soeur Geneviève soeur et novice de Thérèse* [Advice and memories collected by Sister Geneviève—Thérèse's sister and novice]. Trésors du christianisme. Paris: Éditions du Cerf, 2009.

Thérèse of Lisieux. *Histoire d'une âme, manuscrits autobiographiques, Sainte Thérèse de l'Enfant-Jésus et de la Sainte-Face* [Story of a soul, autobiographical manuscripts, Saint Thérèse of the Child Jesus and the Holy Face]. Paris: Éditions du Cerf DDB, 1995.

Vinatier, Jean. *Mère Agnès de Jésus, Pauline Martin soeur aînée et « Petite Mère » de Sainte Thérèse de l'Enfant-Jésus* [Mother Agnès of Jesus, Pauline Martin, Saint Thérèse of the Child Jesus' older sister and "little mother"]. Paris: Éditions du Cerf, 1993.